Feelings and competencies of an M&A

Sergio BRUNO

Feelings and competencies of an M&A

The very soft side of Post Merger Integration

Sergio BRUNO

Feelings and competencies of an M&A

The very soft side of Post Merger Integration

© 2020 Sergio BRUNO

Cover by Lian Lubany

ISBN 978-0-244-57905-0

First edition – May 2020

Printed by:

Lulu Press, Inc.
627 Davis Drive, Suite 300
Morrisville, NC 27560 - U.S.A.
http://www.lulu.com

All rights reserved. No part of this publication may be reproduced, distributed, or transmitted in any form or by any means, including photocopying, recording, or other electronic or mechanical methods, without the prior written permission of the publisher, except in the case of brief quotations embodied in critical reviews and certain other non-commercial uses permitted by copyright law.

To Silvia

Acknowledgements

I would like to thank all the people that helped me to grow up professionally and personally and made me able to write this book.
II would like to thank all my colleagues in GPMIP that motivated me towards this achievement.
I would like to thank Lian for being an artist in all the things she does and Carmen for her curiosity.
I would like to thank all the colleagues, clients, suppliers and competitors I met in my professional life.

Contents

Introduction 5
Part 1: Feelings 11
   Feelings, emotions, passions 13
   The Behaviour of the Consumer............................. 14
   The Behaviour of Companies................................. 17
   Corporate culture... 20
   Feelings during an M&A 21
   (Defensive feelings)... 23
1 Fear... 26
2 Disillusion.. 30
3 Shame.. 33
4 Envy.. 37
   (Active feelings) 42
1 Trust... 43
2 Enthusiasm 48
3 Motivation 52
4 Curiosity.. 58
Part 2: Competencies 61
   What are competencies?.. 63
   Why shall we master competencies?................... 65
1 Problem solving............ *APOLLO 13*................... 66
2 Planning.......................... *THE NEXT 3 DAYS*...... 73
3 Communication .... *+ MARGIN CALL*.......... 81
4 Negotiation................... *THE NEGOTIATOR*....... 88
5 Systemic thinking......... *DR. STRANGELOVE*...... 98

1
+ DON JUAN DEMARCO

6	Situation awareness......*THE DEVIL WEARS PRADA*......106
7	Multicultural thinking......*LOST IN TRANSLATION*......112
8	Focus on goal......*THE PECK + THE MOMMY*......115
9	Managing people......+ *HACKSAW RIDGE*......119

Part 3: Cases & Exercises..................................123
   Robert and the new boss.................................125
   Susan in the matrix 127
   Who is Thomas?..131
   Bob & Jane..133
   Can we have Abhishek back?...........................135
   How to choose your team...............................137
   How to improve your team..............................147

+ GLADIATOR

Every portrait that is painted with feeling is a portrait of the artist, not of the sitter.

Oscar Wilde, The Picture of Dorian Gray

Introduction

I like this quote very much: «Every portrait that is painted with feeling is a portrait of the artist, not of the sitter».
Here we will not draw a portrait (also because we are businesspeople, not artists) nonetheless we will describe what are the colours that are used to paint.

We will talk about what are the feelings that people feel during an M&A. The final picture of the merged company will be a portrait that will be painted using these colours. If you want to have an idea of how the final portrait will look like, I think it can be a good idea to start by looking at the colours that will appear on the canvas.

I should have started with a chapter "Structure of the book", but then I got the feeling that talking about feelings upfront was more important. It is not the most structured way to describe the structure of the book, but I think it works.

Ok, let's be serious.

This book is overall divided into three parts [1].

The first part deals with the feelings that people experience during an M&A

The second part deals with the competencies (soft skills) that are required during an M&A

The third part is a collection of case-exercises. You can use this section as a practical application of what you read before or as a test to see if the author of this book was good in transferring you the concepts.

We are talking about business. This is not a novel. I know. But I really would like to help the reader and to relieve his/her boredom caused by reading a business book. This is the reason why, from time to time, I put some "off the records notes". These notes are written with the lightness and wisdom that come from several years of working with several companies and several people. You can use them as a pause to relax or as a closer look to a reality described without any mask. Or both of them!

> You will recognize them in the book since they are written in this way. A bit smaller font and indented. As if I was whispering into your ears.

---

[1] *This is the way another famous book begins; it was written by Julius Caesar some 2000 years ago.*

Who is the ideal reader that we kept in mind while writing the book?

> Of course, you: if you bought this book and you are reading it, it is self-evident that you are our ideal reader.

This book is for these categories of readers:
1) People who work in the M&A business and want to have a better understanding of the soft side of the M&A
2) People who work in the management consulting business and want to understand better the M&A business
3) People who work in a company that is undergoing or will undergo an M&A
4) Everyone who was expecting a book that deals with the "Pandora box" of the feelings and the soft items in business
5) Students who want to understand this side of the M&A

What is the style of this book?
We did not want to be too boring or too academic.
We preferred to use an "everyday language" in order to make the book easier to read.

Who is "we"?

Sometimes I used "I", sometimes I used "we". Never mind! I'm a management consultant and all management consultant like to jump from the "I" to the "we" and back.
It is always me.

The movie corner. What is it?
We described feelings and we described competencies. We also made a good number of examples. Nonetheless we like to use more than one communication channel. At the end of each chapter, we put a reference to a movie where that feeling or that competency is expressed. If you are not interested or if you haven't seen the movie, you can skip this part. If you have seen the movie, we think you will be pleased to think of it and find in it the feeling or the competency you have just read about.

Not enough!
We are not happy if you just read the book. We want you to make this book your own book. This is why at the end of each feeling or each competency you will find a dedicated page where we will ask you some questions. These questions are intended to help you focus on your specific experiences. Just reading a book is not enough if you really want to improve. The book is a good tool to help you, but

the one that can really change your career or your business is .... You.

Part 1: Feelings

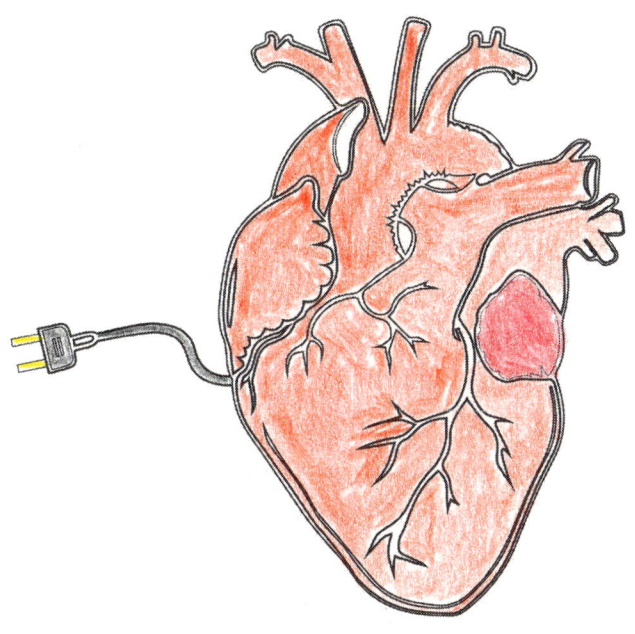

Feelings, emotions, passions

There are different theories about these concepts. Psychanalysis and Psychology taught us a lot about them and their differences. If you are interested in exploring them deeper from a psychological perspective, there are many good books and articles.
Here we want to look at them from a business perspective, we want to focus on how to manage them in a project. Although we are aware that there are differences between them, for the sake of simplicity, here we will use the different words without distinction.

Historically, emotions have always been the fortress of the arts: poetry, music, painting, etc. They gave us wonderful and unforgettable masterpieces describing the sensations that a person feels in a specific situation. Historically there has always been a clear and sharp division between the "world of feelings" and the "word of rationality". Consequently, we grew up in a culture that divides the world in two: on one side there are arts, feelings, etc. on the other side there are thinking, business, work, etc. Let's see some examples.

The Behaviour of the Consumer

The classical economic theory states that if there are two shops "Shop A" and "Shop B" and both are selling the same product but at a different price, the consumer goes to the shop with the lower price.

There is absolutely no reason why consumers should pay 10 EUR for a product when they can have exactly the same product at the price of 9 EUR.

If some consumers buy the product @10 EUR, this is a mistake due to lack of information (they are not aware of the existence of the other shop) or an exception that is irrelevant for the economic theory.

In this economic theory, the shop with the higher price has only two options: reduce the price or go out of the market.

This model cannot explain why many consumers still prefer to buy the same product at a higher price. At a certain point in time, these consumers became too many to be considered as a mistake or an exception.

Then the giant of marketing, Philip Kotler[2], came. Kotler told us that the real world is a bit more

---

[2] *Philip Kotler is the author of the book "Marketing Management" which is considered the founding milestone of modern marketing.*

complex: there are not only two P's (the Product and the Price) but there are also the Place and the Promotion. In other words, the consumer does not make his/her choice only based on the quality of the product and on the price. Consumers can buy the same product at a higher price if they are influenced by the brand, by the advertisement, by the shopping experience, etc.

This represents a first and very important step to make the model of consumer behaviour more complex and more adherent to the real world.

In the real world there are also feelings, emotions, passions. We cannot keep them out!

Consumers prefer to buy in Shop A, paying 10 EUR for the same product that they could buy in Shop B, paying 9 EUR, because the brand of Shop A is better than the brand of Shop B. Or because the shopping experience in Shop A is better that the shopping experience in Shop B. Or the consumer likes (or loves) the owner of Shop A, or because the consumer dislikes (or hates) the owner of Shop B, or because the owner of Shop B has a very nice car and the consumer is envious!

I know, in a traditional business culture we are not used to accept this explanation for the behaviour of a consumer. In traditional business culture, we need to find an explanation that relies on rational, objective and "solid" assumptions.

The world of feelings and the world of business have always been kept rigidly divided.

On one side of the wall there was the world of artists, the only one who could understand feelings and were allowed to talk about feelings.

On the other side of the wall there was the world of business. Many people in business considered feelings a mistake – something to avoid.

This "Emotional division" lasted for many years. People from each side, looked at the people of the other side, as not being able to understand their world.

In the past there have been several attempts to create a breach in this division. Perhaps the best and largest breach was created by Daniel Goleman, with the book he wrote in 1995: "Emotional Intelligence". We are talking about 1995! Not many years ago! No surprise if, even today, talking about feelings in the world of business is still not fully and universally accepted.

Do not forget that many managers and executives started their careers before Goleman's works, when the Emotional division was still untouched.

The Behaviour of Companies

We often read that «a company decided to launch a new product in order to increase its market share», or «another company decided to kill an existing product because the analysis of its product portfolio said to do so».
We read about a company acquiring another company to become a market leader. We also read that two companies decide to merge in order to develop synergies, i.e. reduce costs, i.e. increase profit.

In most cases, these are true.

But there are two things that are often ignored (or not considered enough):

First: Companies are not "alien / inanimate / abstract" entities.
Companies are made of human beings and the decisions are made by human beings (it is either the CEO, the board, owners, managers or executives who make decisions, not "the company").

Second: People working in a company have their own feelings.
This means that when they make decisions, to some degree, these decisions are influenced also by their feelings.

Today we know that feelings cannot be segregated from business. We know that the feelings of a consumer are important. We know that, when we choose between two job opportunities, we make our decision also based on our feelings. We know that when an executive makes a decision, after examining all the data, after tons of meetings, of Excel files, of PowerPoint presentations, he/she makes this decision also based on feelings (we call it "gut-feeling")[3].

Feelings are important in business! We know this. We're aware of it. When we read an article about it, we agree. When we listen to a speech about it, we nod.
Nonetheless, in our intimate soul, we consider the combination of feelings and business still a bit... weird, don't we?

If we read in a business newspaper: «CompanyA acquired CompanyB because CompanyA wanted to increase its market share» we can discuss about the

---

[3] *Do you remember the book "Straight from the gut" by Jack Welch? We are in 2003.*

future of the market, about the price of the acquisition, about other competitors.... nothing strange.

Have you ever read in a business newspaper: «The owners of CompanyA acquired CompanyB because they were envious of the owners of CompanyB»? or «The owners of CompanyA acquired CompanyB because they were afraid of the owners of CompanyB»? or «The owners of CompanyA acquired CompanyB because they have a big ego»?

Someone can tell you: «These are things that you do not read in newspapers, because they are not true!»

Maybe this is correct ... or maybe it means that we are not yet mature enough to accept it and to put at the same level of importance a rational, fact-based decision and an emotional, feeling-based decision.

Corporate culture

Modern management approaches give feelings the importance they deserve.
We created an expression to express the combination of feelings, values, beliefs, etc.
We call this "corporate culture".
The concept of corporate culture is now well established and accepted in the business world everywhere.
Well... almost everywhere, believe me...

«You cannot produce a change in any organization, if you do not consider a cultural change».

This statement is mostly accepted everywhere. But we can dig a bit deeper. We can explore the world of feelings that is behind corporate culture.
We can explore how people in a company feel.
And we can do this during a time of big change, for example when the company acquires another company, is acquired by another company, or when two companies merge together.

We can explore the feelings of people during an M&A.

Feelings during an M&A

Do not worry! We are not going into the field of psychoanalysis here!

> Also because we would not be able to come out!

We'll focus on the feelings that people have during an M&A, in particular during a post-merger integration (PMI) project. We will explore how feelings impact the progress of the integration project itself and how we can manage them.

Emotional agility is needed for M&A success.
You will always have emotions, even in the business world.
It's important to understand how to deal with emotions: both our emotions and the emotions of people we are working with.
Mergers and acquisitions imply a big change and, therefore, it moves a lot of emotions.
To manage an M&A project, you must have a certain level of "emotional agility" – the emotions behind how leaders perform and how they treat others at the

workplace. Understanding this will move you and your team towards M&A success.

In our experience, we've found a certain set of feelings play out rather often during an Integration project. We divided this huge and complex world of feeling into two categories:
- Defensive feelings
- Active feeling

Defensive feelings

The defensive category is the most widespread. We can easily understand why: in many cases an M&A is the event that implies the biggest changes in an organization.

Today we live in a complex world, where there are many things than can cause or produce a change. We call these things "drivers" of change. Here is a short list of drivers of change:
- technology,
- globalization,
- regulatory, and many others.

For example, how technology is a driver of change? Think, for example, of what happened with the development of mobile communications: people now can work remotely from home, whilst before your professional life was only at the office, and home was kept for your family life only.

How globalisation is a driver of change? Think of a company based in Europe, with suppliers in Asia and clients in America: they must speak three (or more) different languages. Before the globalisation their life was completely different.

We could continue with the examples, but I would like to ask you this question: «how long do these drivers take to produce a change?» You can say that these drivers changed our lives quickly, but they took at least some years.

An M&A produces changes in a much shorter period of time!
It is palpable to people that the way they work, the way they spend 8 hours (or more) a day changes overnight!

The employees of a company start hearing some rumours at the coffee machine saying that their company will merge with another company. It is still a rumour. There is nothing official. But people start feeling something strange in their stomach. And then, the deal is announced, and the merger will happen effectively from next week.

It is rather normal that when you face these changes in a very short time, you are scared and you try defending yourself, your job, your world, etc. This is the reason why we called these feelings "defensive feelings".

No surprise if people have these defensive feelings, but a good manager must consider this!

When people in a company adopt a defensive behaviour, the company cannot be changed just by making structural changes. You need to dig a bit deeper and use your Emotional Intelligence to understand the reasons behind their behaviour.

If a manager does not pay attention to these defensive feelings, they can quickly generate some behaviours that are very dangerous for the success of the project.

In the following chapters we will explore more in detail the most common among these defensive feelings and we will see how to deal with them.

The most common defensive feelings are:
-   Fear
-   Disillusion
-   Shame
-   Envy

Fear

«I'm afraid I'm not doing my job right»;
«Why I was not invited to the meeting? »;
«Am I going to be fired? »;

Fear was - historically - a good and useful feeling. Fear was a normal reaction towards something that we perceived as dangerous and it was supposed to prepare our body prepared for fighting the danger or escaping from the danger. Think, for a moment, of our ancestors, in a context where they were facing a fierce tiger! They had just two options: escape or fight.

In our time, in the working environment, the context is much more complex. There are dangers, but the reaction to the danger cannot be simply: escape or fight.
Many times, the reaction requires thinking, analysing, discussing, etc. All these actions require a focused mindset not a nervous and anxious one.

In our time, fear, very often, brings us to rush decisions (that are often wrong) just because we have the urge to escape from the danger. This is an example of the use of the "escape" toolkit: the same toolkit that was developed when our ancestors had to escape from the tiger. Here of course the use of this toolkit brings us – generally – to a misguided solution.

Other times fear makes us attack a colleague or a client (!) because we perceive him/her as dangerous and we want to attack before being attacked. Again, this is an example of the use of the "attack" toolkit in a misguided situation.

A good employee should develop self-control in order to manage fear and to avoid fear degenerates from a normal feeling to a critical situation such as panic or depression.

Good managers must develop self-control, as all the other employees, but this is not enough.
They must develop the ability to recognise in the employees what is behind some behaviours.

If an employee attacks another employee, maybe this is not a "normal" attack, it is just an expression of the feeling of fear.
If we are in this situation, the manager should not work on the symptom (the attack) but on the cause (the feeling of fear).

The manager must not say: «you should not attack your colleagues! » but «what are you afraid of? ».

 ## The movie corner

The Silence of the Lambs
Directed by Jonathan Demme
USA 1991

Whenever you ask: «name me a movie that evokes the feeling of fear», most people answer «The Silence of the Lambs».
Not much more to say... just watch it if you haven't or think of it if you have... and tell me what you feel

 **Make this book your book**

Think of a situation where you lived this feeling

....
....

Think of a situation where someone close to you lived this feeling

....
....

What did you do?

....
....

What will you change / what will you do next time?

....
....

Disillusion

«We have tried it several times...»;
«After this merger, things will remain the same»;
«It is better to do nothing; I'll just wait and see what happens to my job».

This is the feeling of disillusion.
This feeling brings laziness. Even worse: it can bring loneliness. If the integration project takes-off, people with this feeling can isolate themselves from the rest of the team and will no longer provide their contribution to the project.

In the best-case scenario, you are losing their help; in the worst case, they could even influence negatively other people. This feeling can spread around the company.

This feeling – more than other ones – is very contagious.

The symptoms are less evident than fear, since the employees will continue working as if nothing happened apparently. The employees will not show anything openly. They will just complain silently, something like a groan.

The employees who were engaged in the project, hearing their groans, day after day, will lose their motivation and then disillusion spreads like the black death.

The manger must pay a lot of attention to the weak signals and intercept any feeling of disillusion before they spread among the company.
Then the manager must work very carefully with the disillusioned employee, maybe with some ad hoc sessions in order to re-establish his/her right motivation level.

 **The movie corner**

Easy Rider
Directed by Dennis Hopper
USA 1969

A very "strong" movie. A picture of a disillusioned society in the late 60's

 **Make this book your book**

Think of a situation where you lived this feeling

....
....

Think of a situation where someone close to you lived this feeling

....
....

What did you do?

....
....

What will you change / what will you do next time?

....
....

Shame

Shame is very much influenced by culture. Not only the corporate culture we talked about previously, but also the culture of the community, the group or even the country.
This must be considered carefully in cross-border M&A, particularly with western/eastern companies.
For example, in the Japanese culture, this feeling is very strong. Pay attention in giving negative feedback to a Japanese colleague: the reaction you produce can be much bigger that what could happen with a western colleague.

Shame is a pain we feel when we perceive that our social esteem has been damaged.

We think that other people have a bad opinion of us. Sometimes we could even think to attack them.
An example is when some people, in a meeting, do not know something important for the understanding of the discussion. They feel ashamed to ask. They are afraid to lose credibility in front of the colleagues. They do not ask and so they do not understand 100% the discussion and therefore they cannot give useful contributions.

The worst-case scenario is when they say the meeting was useless and they attack the people involved or the decisions taken during the meeting.

When a manager works with people with this feeling, the manager must always:
- pay attention to the social esteem of the team towards these people
- treat this social esteem as a very fragile crystal glass.

Sometimes the manager must anticipate any situation that could attempt the social esteem. In the example of the meeting before, the manager could have made an introduction giving all the details required to be fully aware of the situation. In this way no one would have needed to ask or feel ashamed to ask.

Another technique the manager can use is to be the first one to ask questions, even if the manager knows already the answer, just to avoid any awkward situation that might appear. For example, during a meeting, when someone uses an acronym, the manager could ask «can you please tell me what that acronym means? », even if the manager knows the meaning of the acronym without asking.

 # The movie corner

Meet the Parents
Directed by Jay Roach
USA 2000

We chose a comedy film here since "shame" is a feeling people don't like and we wanted to lighten the mood.
It is the story of a young man who wants to propose to his girlfriend. He meets her parents and they do everything they can to make him feel ashamed.

 **Make this book your book**

Think of a situation where you lived this feeling

....
....

Think of a situation where someone close to you lived this feeling

....
....

What did you do?

....
....

What will you change / what will you do next time?

....
....

Envy

Envy is one of the most dangerous feelings. For two reasons:

1) When an envious colleague sees another colleague attain something or reach an objective, the envious colleague is not looking at what the other colleague has done to reach that goal; he/she concentrates at what can be done to sabotage the colleague, to make the colleague lose what they just got.

2) Envy is one of the most denied feelings. Some people can admit they feel fear, or even anger; but very few (if any) will admit he/she feels envious towards a colleague. There is a sort of "corporate shame" that prevents envy to be communicated openly.

It is important to investigate the root causes that generate this feeling, so that we can fight it or avoid it.

Envy is born when there is the coexistence of two factors:
- low self esteem

- perception of injustice

Let's explore better.

The envious colleague perceives himself/herself as weaker, less skilled or – generally - inferior colleague. He/she thinks he/she lacks something to be equal to other colleagues.
Be careful: this is all about how he/she perceives, not about what is true.

The envious colleague thinks he/she suffered a form of injustice. The injustice can derive from everywhere:
- inside the company from the boss or another colleague.
- outside the company from relatives or friends.

The good news is that both these causes must coexist to trigger this feeling.
If there is only low self-esteem, we could find disillusion.
If there is only perception of injustice, we could find anger.

The bad news is that, when both causes are present, we have a ticking bomb, ready to explode.

What are the countermeasures?

We can defuse both triggering causes or, at least, one of them.

We can work on low self-esteem by enforcing skills, competences, by making the employee gain a certificate in a subject that is useful for his/her job. By asking him/her to speak in front of his/her colleagues about what he/she discovered...

We can work on the perception of an injustice by creating an environment where differences among employees are accepted and welcomed.
Organise inclusive events outside the company, after working hours.
Encourage people to speak frankly to you, in your office, if something happened they do not like.

 **The movie corner**

Amadeus
Directed by Miloš Forman
USA 1984

The movie tells the story of the composer Wolfgang Amadeus Mozart. In the movie the story is told by

Antonio Salieri. Salieri was the official composer of the emperor, a very important (and well paid) job. Mozart was a young composer without any official role. The movie represents very well a situation where we have one person (Salieri) with a hierarchical power and another person (Mozart) with less power but much cleverer. Salieri had a musical competency that was just enough to realise that Mozart was a genius and this made him very envious. Does this remind you of any situation you lived while working on a project?

 **Make this book your book**

Think of a situation where you lived this feeling

....
....

Think of a situation where someone close to you lived this feeling

....
....

What did you do?

....
....

What will you change / what will you do next time?

....
....

Active feelings

In the previous chapters we started with the defensive category since that category is, generally, common between both people of the acquired company and people of the acquiring company.
Even people in the acquiring company could feel fear of the changes implied by the organisation change, or they could feel envious towards a colleague who made a big career move.

The active category, on the other hand, is generally found only among people of the acquiring company, so these feelings are – unfortunately – somehow more difficult to find.

The most common active feelings are:
- Trust
- Enthusiasm
- Motivation
- Curiosity

Trust

There are two types of trust:

1) Trust towards the future: it is the feeling that makes us do something because we think (we trust) that what we are doing now will bring us good in the future.

2) Trust towards a person: the feeling that makes us share our thoughts (or our feelings) with a colleague (or any person) without the fear of being betrayed.

If you like to paint a picture with your imagination, we can say that the feeling of trust is a sort of bridge that goes from us to something or someone else. It is a bridge suspended over a gap.

This feeling is quite powerful and very useful for the success of any project aiming at producing a change in the company.

People with this feeling trust the fact that what they are doing now, the late hours in the office, working some weekends, will bring them some good in the future. The good can be a promotion or a salary increase or a bonus or a public recognition for what they did or anything else they like.

People with this feeling trust their colleagues, trust each other. They are 100% sure that if they do any mistake, their colleagues will help them and will not sell them out.

> Hard to believe?
> I know... but there are not only defensive feelings, I told you!

Since this feeling -as you can imagine- is very powerful, the manager must feed it as much as possible!

The strange thing is that the best food for trust is ... trust itself!

You must give trust if you want to build trust.
And do not even think to play both sides.

If cannot promise something, simply do not promise it!

Do not say: «if you do well, then you will be promoted» if you do not have the full control over the promotion path.
If the promotion of one of your employees depends also on the overall performance of the company or

depends on the new promotion policies that the Human Resources Department will publish next month, you do not have the full control over the promotion path.
Accept the fact that your power in the company has a limit!
You should say: «if you do well, then I will do all what is my power to make you get your well-deserved promotion»

 **The movie corner**

Million Dollar Baby
Directed by Clint Eastwood
USA 2004

It is the story of a boxing trainer who accepts to train a young girl while she learns to trust him.

The Hunt for Red October
Directed by John McTiernan
USA 1990

We are on a submarine. An enemy has just launched a torpedo towards us. Instead of trying to avoid the torpedo the commander of the submarine orders to go full speed towards the torpedo itself. He knows that by doing so the torpedo will not have enough time get ready to explode during the collision. A good example of trust when the submarine's team follows the order of the commander.

 # Make this book your book

Think of a situation where you lived this feeling

....
....

Think of a situation where someone close to you lived this feeling

....
....

What did you do?

....
....

What will you change / what will you do next time?

....
....

Enthusiasm

Another very powerful feeling!
Someone calls it "flow", like the flow that motivates and moves people towards the goal.

It is the feeling that makes you say: «Yes, we can do it!».
It is the feeling that makes you think: «The distance between our dream and our reality is just our action»

The unexperienced manager could think: «ok, perfect! I have a team of enthusiastic people, they will do their job in a flash, I can rest and simply wait for the job to be completed»

This a very common mistake unexperienced managers do.

Experienced managers know they must achieve two important goals:

First goal:
The feeling of enthusiasm is a fire that stops burning very quickly if something wrong happens.

The managers must keep the way clear, so that this feeling can make the wheels of the project run smooth and fast.

Second goal:
This feeling makes people move and move fast.
Several times people feel enthusiastic in doing a job even if this job is not exactly the top priority of the project.
So, the manager must direct and channel this flow towards something that is actually useful for the project.

And now comes the big challenge for the manager:
The two goals above are – generally – contradictory: if you focus on the first, then you miss the second and vice versa.

Think of a colleague who starts working on something, full of enthusiasm; unfortunately, what this colleague is doing is ultimately useless for the project... what can the manager do:

Option a: tell the employee «great, you are doing well, well done! »
This will reach the first goal but will lead very far from the second goal

Option b: tell the employee «please stop doing this, you should focus on that instead»
This is very good for the second goal, but you will destroy the feeling of enthusiasm and go far away from the first goal

So, what is the right solution?
Think carefully of the way you give feedbacks and give feedbacks at the right time!

> I know, you thought that having an enthusiastic team meant you had the immediate solution to the project in your pocket... and now you hate me since I told you it is not so...

 **The movie corner**

Scent of a Woman
Directed by Martin Brest
USA 1992

The movie is a remake of a 1974 movie with a very similar story. It deals with a man who is blind and, despite this disability, he wants to live his life to the fullest.

 # Make this book your book

Think of a situation where you lived this feeling

....
....

Think of a situation where someone close to you lived this feeling

....
....

What did you do?

....
....

What will you change / what will you do next time?

....
....

Motivation

This is the "old brother" of enthusiasm.
In the previous chapter we said that enthusiasm is like a fire, a big fire that produces a lot of heat, but it can burn out rather quickly.
Would it be possible to have another fire, a fire that is smaller but that lasts longer?
Yes, it is possible. It is motivation.

Motivation is more complex than enthusiasm.
If you like a very romantic comparison, we could say that enthusiasm is like "falling in love" and motivation is like "staying in love".

Let's set romance aside and get back to business.

A manager must make sure that the people working with him/her on his/her project have a good amount of motivation.

In order to have people with a good amount of motivation, the manager must understand what are the pipes that bring the oil to the long burning fire of the motivation.

What are these pipes?

There are many, here are some examples:

The oldest and easiest way to motivate your team is to give them a good amount of money.
But, do not over-simplify!
Money does not mean the same thing for everyone.
Or it is not as important for everyone.

Other people, for example, give a lot of importance to work-life balance. They are more sensitive towards the opportunity to go home early in the evening than towards having an increase in compensation.

Other people get crazy for personal visibility. They want to take centre stage. They like to have the attention in a meeting and present the progress of the project.

Other people like to have a good relationship with their colleagues. That kind of relationship where you don't need to protect yourself every day.

Other people love to increase their knowledge and feel happy when the company sends them to a training course.

We could go on with different examples.

Of course, the ideal solution would be:
give a lot of money to your team,
+ give them the opportunity to have a good work-life balance
+ give them a lot of personal visibility
+ give them an environment with wonderful relationships
+ give them all the training they want
+ ...

Unfortunately, you can have this list realised fully only in fairy tales.

In the real world, you have to choose.
You can pump oil only into one pipe.

> If you are unlucky you cannot pump oil into any pipe, since you don't have any oil.

Pumping oil into any of the pipes is expensive.
Giving your team more money is clearly expensive.
Letting them go home early in the evening is expensive in the same way
And so on.

So, the question for the manager is:

Which pipe should I pump the oil into?

For the success of my project, is it more effective if I let one of my team members go home early or if I give him/her the opportunity to take centre stage at the next meeting?

How can I use the cards that I have in my hands to produce the largest amount of motivation among my team members?

To answer these questions, you must consider the following three rules.

First rule:
Understand the real needs of each individual of your team.

Second rule:
Consider that each person has his/her own pipes. "One-size-fits-all" is a tremendous mistake.

Third rule:
A person could change his/her pipes during his/her life. Don't assume that a pipe that was good 3 years ago, still is.

 **The movie corner**

The Mission
Directed by Roland Joffé
United Kingdom 1986

The title itself tells already a lot! It tells the story of the work done by several people near Iguazu Falls describing how they fight against all sorts of difficulties

 # Make this book your book

Think of a situation where you lived this feeling

....
....

Think of a situation where someone close to you lived this feeling

....
....

What did you do?

....
....

What will you change / what will you do next time?

....
....

Curiosity

We mean curiosity in the broadest sense. Curiosity is the feeling that makes you wake up in the morning and explore the new day.
Curiosity is the feeling than makes you stay in the project and see what will happen, how the integration will end.

Curiosity is the feeling that makes you learn. It is the feeling that makes you ask in a meeting «Hey, can we try this? » or «Could we see what happens if we change this? ».

It's easier to find curiosity in junior employees who are hungry to learn. Unfortunately, this is the reason why "having the hungry feeling of curiosity" is often confused with "being a junior and unexperienced".

This is a very big mistake!

It was hard to make managers aware of this mistake till when a guy from Cupertino (California) in a famous public speech invited everyone to «stay hungry and foolish[4]».

After that speech, curiosity was very much more welcome!

 **The movie corner**

The Theory of Everything
Directed by James Marsh
United Kingdom / Japan / United States 2014

The movie deals with the life of the theoretical physicist Stephen Hawking. It is a very good representation of his curiosity that made him continue his researches against any difficulty.

---

[4] *It was the speech called "Commencement address" given in June 2005 at Stanford University by Steve Jobs*

 # Make this book your book

Think of a situation where you lived this feeling

....
....

Think of a situation where someone close to you lived this feeling

....
....

What did you do?

....
....

What will you change / what will you do next time?

....
....

Part 2: Competencies

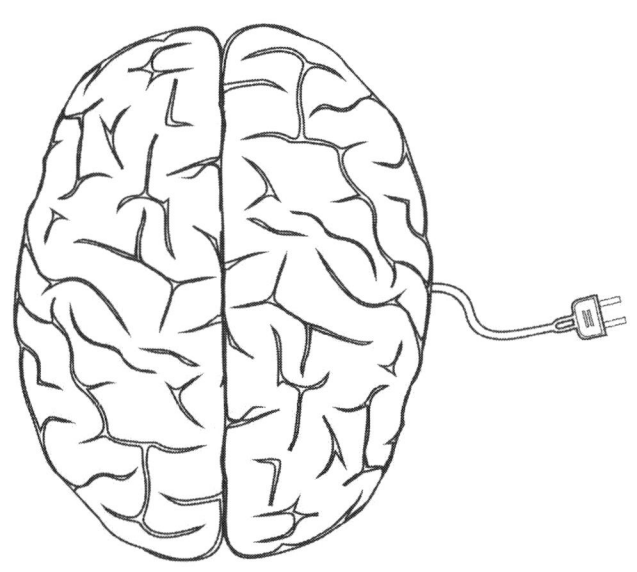

What are competencies?

By "competencies" we mean "management competencies" or a set of "soft" skills. We do not mean "hard" skills or "technical" skills.
Just to give an example: knowing the accounting rules of the IFRS[5] is a hard skill.
Knowing how to solve a problem is a competency.
There are tons of books that deal with the topic of competencies. And this is good because it means that there are more and more companies who became aware of the importance of competencies!
At the same time, we must admit that there is not a unique classification of these competencies: different authors gave different names to the same competency or classified them in a different way etc.

Here we will focus on the specific set of competencies that are required for an integration project and we will provide a pragmatic definition of these competencies.
By "pragmatic definition" we mean that we will not define the competencies in a theoretical abstract

---

[5] *IFRS is an acronym that refers to a system that the accountants use to prepare the financial statements of a company.*

way, but we will define them by providing some examples of actions.

Let me give you an example.
We will not say that "Problem Solving" is «the ability to find a solution to a general problem in a difficult situation mobilising the right people at the right time». This is a nice definition, but it does not bring you anywhere.
We will say that «you have the Problem-Solving competency if you do this specific set of actions in your professional life». Do not be impatient! We will give you the complete set of actions in a few pages. (if you cannot resist, you can jump to the "Problem Solving chapter).
This set of specific actions is what we mean by "pragmatic definition". It comes from the ancient Greek "pragma" which means "your actions".
In the next few pages, we will describe each competency with more detail.
In the description we will provide a list of actions. We will use the form: "Bob does this"; "Mary does that". Of course, we are not referring to any Bob or Mary in particular! We preferred to use a specific name to keep it simply. Otherwise we should have used the form "He/she does this" which we find a bit more impersonal and boring.

Why shall we master competencies?

There are several reasons.

Let's start from this one: you must choose which one of your teammates is the best to work with you on the Post Merger Integration project. How can you make this selection?

Let's suppose that you have a budget that you must spend on training. How will you spend this budget?

Understanding how competencies work give you a framework that can be very useful to answer these questions.

> If these questions scared you, or if you know the answer but you would like to refresh it, you can go to section 3 of this book.

Problem solving

Problem solving is the most famous competency.
In every project in every job, everywhere, I have always found it.

> I have also found it in every résumé I received. It is so common that everyone has it. Or pretend to have it. Unfortunately.

Maybe because managing a company or a project involves solving problems...

Let's start with the list of actions that define this competency with our "friend" Bob.

1. Bob Analyses the situation.

2. Bob puts on the table a set of potential solution (we said: «a set», that is more than 1).
3. Bob evaluates pros and cons of each potential solution.

4. Bob makes a decision: he picks one potential solution.

5. Bob checks if the solution he picked solves the problem. If not, he iterates from the beginning.

6. Bob checks if the problem was a one-off problem or a recurring problem.

7. If it is a recurring problem, then Bob ensures that, with the solution he picked, this problem will not show in the future. If not, he iterates from the beginning.

8. Once Bob found the final solution, he writes down what he did. We say he creates a knowledge base documenting the solution.

If you like the flow charts, here you are welcome!

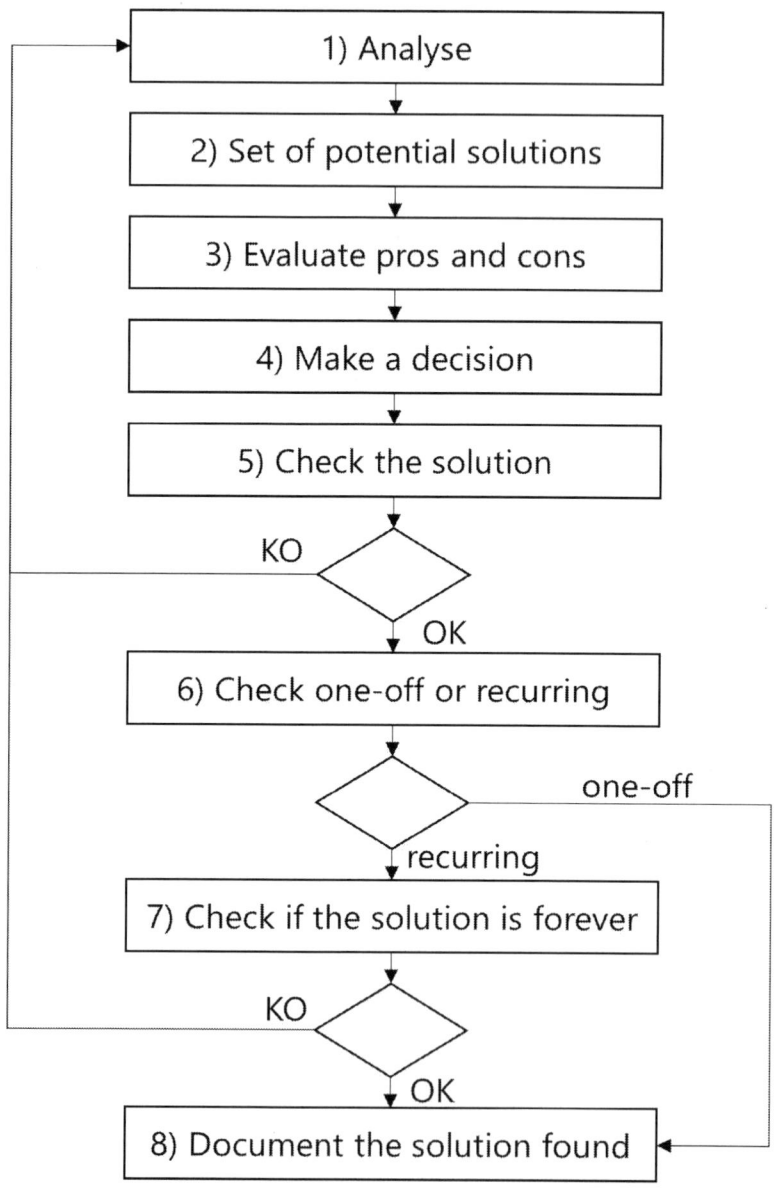

When you look at the flow chart it looks so easy, nonetheless each step hides a huge trap. Let's see why.

1. Some people forget to analyse the situation jumping directly to the conclusion. Generally, this happens when people feel the pressure of the clock ticking and they feel the need to give a solution as soon as possible, whatever it is, just to stop the ticking clock.

2. Some people stop the search when they have one (just one) solution. This is wrong since it prevents you from looking at the situation from different perspectives. How can you ever know if the solution found was the best one if it was the only one?

3. The evaluation of pros and cons is based on what is good for the entire company, or on what is good for me (and only me)? Besides, choice is made on what is really good or on who proposed the solution?

4. Make a decision! Come on! If you stop here, you just made a good analysis. You must take the risk of picking one of the solutions. You cannot foresee the future, but no one else can! Do not be afraid.

5. Do not leave the battlefield before the battle is over, completely over! Are you sure that the solution you found was really a solution?

6. A company needs a complete solution that makes all clients happy, not a partial solution that makes just one client happy. If the problem can occur again tomorrow, we cannot restart everything, it is too expensive.

7. So, does this solution work well for all the possible situations or it cover us just in one case leaving us at risk in all other cases?

8. Tomorrow you can receive a very good offer from another company, or you can retire. The company should not let your knowledge go away completely with you. The company must ask you to document what you did, the analyses you made, how you choose that solution etc.
Every company has its own way of documenting things: from a pencil and paper to a huge Artificial Intelligence software.
All of them are good. As long as they are used.

 # The movie corner

Apollo 13
Directed by Ron Howard
USA 1995

«Houston, we have a problem» everyone remembers this sentence from this movie. The sentence has become so famous that sometimes we forget about the movie and just use it when we want to tell our boss that we are experiencing a problem, but we also want to add some "light flavour" to the sentence.

Apollo 13 is the name of a lunar mission. When the team has almost reached the moon, they find a problem, A big one. They decide to come back to Earth, but oxygen is not enough…. And they have to learn problem solving very quickly.

 # Make this book your book

Think of a situation you lived where this competency is required

....
....

What did you do?

....
....

Think to someone you know that, in your opinion, masters this competency

....
....

What will you change / what will you do nest time?

....
....

Planning

1. Omar splits the overall assignment into tasks and analyses them.

2. Omar prioritizes the tasks.

3. Omar puts the task on a work plan.

4. Omar keeps the plan up to date.

«What is the importance of having a plan?»
I know it can sound weird, but I have been asked this question several times at the beginning of an integration project.

Some companies have a structured way of working: they have a written procedure for almost everything that you have to do.
If you recall the chapter "Corporate culture", we can say that these companies have a structured culture
These are the companies that understand easily the value of a plan.

Other companies have a much more "free-hand" culture. They say: «ok let's start the project, then we will see what happens».

The second approach has some advantages.

The first and obvious advantage is that you save all the time and money that should have been spent in the planning activity.

The second advantage is that, since day 1, you start "real" integration activities, you focus on specific real issues.

The third advantage is that you give other people (and your boss in particular) the impression that you have done so many projects like this in the past that you know every step by memory; you don't need a plan since you have the plan in your mind.

> Do you remember Wolfgang Amadeus Mozart? Ha had the music in his mind, before even writing it down on a piece of paper!

Unfortunately, your boss (or the mother company) has a structured culture, so you decide to spend some time in preparing a plan, just to please them.

Since the plan is done only for this reason, you dedicate for the planning activity only a very small amount of time.

I forgot to tell you something general about competencies. Probably this is the right moment to tell you.

If you don't master a competency you cannot understand the benefits that competency brings.

Sometimes you happen to meet people who can only see the advantages of not spending the right amount of time in planning. This is a clear symptom that they don't have the planning competency.

What are the advantages of spending the right amount of time in planning before starting the "real" work?

After Omar split the overall assignment into tasks he was able to understand better what must be done, had the opportunity to delegate some tasks to some of his team mates, realised from the very beginning what were the needs, what the major issues were and what the major risks were.
In other words, he got ready for his job in the right and effective way.

If you are aware that a risk can happen and you take the right countermeasures at the right time, the impact of the risk will be much smaller.
If you wait for the risk to happen and only then you act, then the cost will be much higher.

The time in analysing tasks is an investment for the future life of the project.
Omar prioritizes the tasks because completing all the tasks right now is impossible or too expensive.
Omar decides what must be done now and what must be done later.
This means that he dedicates time in understanding the importance of each single tasks.
What happens if we cannot do this task now? What are the consequences on other tasks?
What are the consequences on the success of the integration project?
These are the questions Omar asks himself. Or his boss, or his teammates.

Once Omar prioritized the tasks, he can apply them to a plan. This is the plan for the integration project. The plan can answer some questions like: «when will the integration project be finished? »

Have you ever heard this question?
What do you think could happen if the answer is: «we started to work on "real activities" immediately,

we decided not to waste time in planning, we have no idea when we will finish»?

I would not be in the shoes of the person who gives this answer to a Board of Directors who invested a certain million EUR in the acquisition of a company.

This person realises that the answer «we have no idea about the end date» could have an "unwelcome impact" on his/her career...
A workaround for this awkward situation could be to invent a date out of the blue and tell everyone they will end the project by that date.

In this way they can exit the meeting with the Board without an immediate "unwelcome impact" on their careers.
But the problem has just been postponed. One month later, that date out of the blue will prove to be completely unrealistic. And what do you think will happen?

I suspect that the "unwelcome impact" on the career will be even more unwelcome.

«What is the value of planning at the beginning of the project if later, during the project, things may change? »

Another common objection.

The plan written at the beginning of the project is not written in stone.
It can be updated! Sorry: it must be updated!

Of course, at the beginning of the project we have a certain level of information. Now, after one month, we have a better understanding and we can say that this task is going to take more time, so that tasks must be postponed, but that other tasks are going to take less time, etc.

This adjustment activity must be done with a reasonable frequency, maybe once or twice a week for example.

This provides you an updated situation of where the project is, what are the critical steps etc.

«Can I take a couple of weeks for holidays? »

If one of your teammates asks you this question, you can easily answer:

«yes, you can, enjoy! » or
«sorry, you can't, you can see according to the plan that your work is fundamental now; could you take your holidays next month? »

The updated plan will help you in managing your team.
Some managers cancel all the holidays for everybody, even those who are not involved in the project, you can never tell...

This is the typical approach when you don't have a plan.

No wonder why these managers never find clever people willing to work with them.

 **The movie corner**

The next three days
Directed by Paul Haggis
USA 2010

It is the story of a woman who is –wrongly- convicted of murdering her boss and is sentenced to life in prison. Her husband organises a very detailed plan to break her out of prison.

 **Make this book your book**

Think of a situation you lived where this competency is required

....
....

What did you do?

....
....

Think to someone you know that, in your opinion, masters this competency

....
....

What will you change / what will you do nest time?

....
....

Communication

Communication is another cornerstone. You find it in all the recruitment ads that you read.
> As a consequence, this is another competency that you will find in all the résumés that you receive.

Communication is important and is becoming more and more important.
Today, management books say that a good manager must invest in communication activities a large percentage of his/her working time.
Some say 50%, other say 70%, other 80%. Anyway... quite a lot.

Let's see what William, our expert in communication does:

1. William listens.

2. William asks questions.

3. Williams makes a summary at the end to check if he understood correctly.

4. William speaks the language of the audience.

5. William verifies that the message has been understood and internalized.

Did you notice the first activity?
William listens.
William, as every good communicator starts by listening, then he asks questions if he does not understand something, then, from time to time, he makes a quick wrap-up to double check if he understood correctly.

I have seen many times, during meetings, people do emails on the PC, messages on the smartphone or draws strange pictures on a piece of paper...
This is not listening. This is just hearing. But hearing is not enough to say that you are communicating.

If you want to communicate you must empty your mind from everything you are thinking about and you must focus on everything that the other person is saying.

If these things are important and you cannot take them off your mind, don't worry. Take your time, finish these things and devote yourself to communication after you have finished.

We mean "listen" in a wide sense.

It is not only the sound of the words. It is everything that revolves around the words.

If William receives an email, Williams looks at who is in the "TO" field, who is the "CC" field, etc.
Then William asks himself «why an email and not a phone call or a meeting in person? ».
«What is behind the choice of this specific medium (the email) instead of another one? ».

If William receives a phone call, he listens not only to the words but also to the tone, etc.

If William meets someone in person, William pays attention to the gestures, to the way the other person is dressed, etc.

This is what we mean by "William listens"

Some people say that in today's hectic way of working, people are getting nervous because no one listens to them.
If you just accomplish the first activity of this competency, you are already half done!

When we say that William speaks the language of the audience, we mean something more than just speaking English if the audience speaks English or German if the audience speaks German.

We mean that if the audience uses a jargon, William uses the same jargon. And if the audience does not use any jargon or any acronym, William does the same.

If the audience uses flowery language, William uses a flowery language.
If the audience uses casual language, William uses a casual language.

The last activity on the list is very important.
William checks that the message has been understood and internalized.

I remember once a manager (Lucy) sent an email to a colleague (Scarlett) and then Lucy told me: «ok, job done! I sent an email to Scarlett; I have completed my task».
What happens if Scarlet does not read the email? Or Scarlett reads the email, but she does not understand what Lucy meant? Or Scarlett reads the email, understands it, but does not agree with it and so does not follow up?

William does not cancel the task from his to-do list after sending an email. Williams checks that the receiver has received, understood, internalized the email.

The sender of the email is accountable for the fact that the receiver follows up.

 **The movie corner**

Margin call
Directed by J. C. Chandor
USA 2011

It is the story of an unnamed investment bank (maybe Lehman Brothers?) during the initial stages of the financial crisis of 2007– 2008.
A junior analyst realised that the bank was going to face a very difficult situation, so he informs his boss, who in turn informs his boss and so on, until they reached the bank's #1 guy.
There is a meeting with everybody involved, from the junior analyst to the #1.
During this meeting the junior analyst tries to explain the situation to the #1 who does not understand and asks him: «Please speak as you might to a young child
or a golden retriever».
This is an example of the importance of communication at all levels: if you have a wonderful

research in your hands but you can't communicate it only with a technical jargon, your work is almost useless.

Don Juan DeMarco
Directed by Jeremy Leven
USA 1995
There is a wonderful scene where a psychiatrist dissuades a would-be suicide who claims to be Don Juan. Pay attention to how the psychiatrist speaks the same language of his counterpart.

 # Make this book your book

Think of a situation you lived where this competency is required

....
....

What did you do?

....
....

Think to someone you know that, in your opinion, masters this competency

....
....

What will you change / what will you do nest time?

....
....

Negotiation

The old school of negotiation says that negotiating is somehow like cheating your counterpart.

This idea was based on a very short focused assumption: you must reach the target in the shortest time, who cares if you ruin the relationship.

«The important thing is to push the client to buy today, who cares if tomorrow we will lose the client». This was the old school.

Today's management community rose the bar. A good negotiator (we will call him Harper here), must work on two sides:
- the side of the target (this was the only side in the old school)
- the side of the relationship

To be more specific: a negotiator that reaches the goal but ruins the relationship is a bad negotiator.

If you like fruits, you will like this example.
A good negotiator is someone who picks the apple and takes care of the apple tree.

Harper picks the apple (he reaches the goal) and takes care of the apple tree (the relationship).

So, what does Harper do?

1. Harper studies the counterpart.

2. Harper define a multidimensional solution.

3. Harper defines his BATNA[6].

4. Harper closes the agreement.

5. Harper makes the counterpart appreciate the agreement.

The first 3 actions must be done before the entering the negotiation.

There is a famous business game where you have CompanyA and CompanyB who both need to buy oranges. The oranges are limited, so both companies rise the price offered for the oranges to secure enough oranges.

---

[6] *We will tell you in a moment what this acronym means*

Then Harper the negotiator arrives, studies the counterparts and discovers that CompanyA just needed the juice of the oranges and CompanyB just needed the peel of the oranges, so there was no need to enter competition, raise the price, etc.

This is a good example of what is "study the counterpart". Understand what the counterpart really needs, put yourself in their shoes.

Second action: define a multidimensional solution.
Let's clarify with a very simple example on price negotiation.
You want to sell a product to one of your counterparts.

The basic approach is a back and forth on the price as you see in this picture:

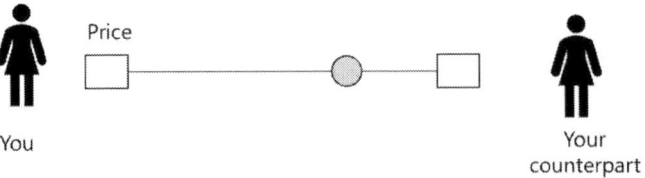

You   Your counterpart

There is just one slider, you will pull the ball towards you, your counterpart will do the opposite. It is like a tug of war.

Maybe at the end you will find a compromise.
But a compromise is just a place in between the two positions; it is not the best solution.
You wanted 100, your counterpart wanted 80, you agree on 90.
You are losing 10, your counterpart is losing 10.
Both of you will go back home with bad taste in your mouth.
Maybe next time you will not be willing to meet again, recalling the last negotiation.

What if we think about a wide range of other dimensions?
In the following pictures we mapped seven dimensions.

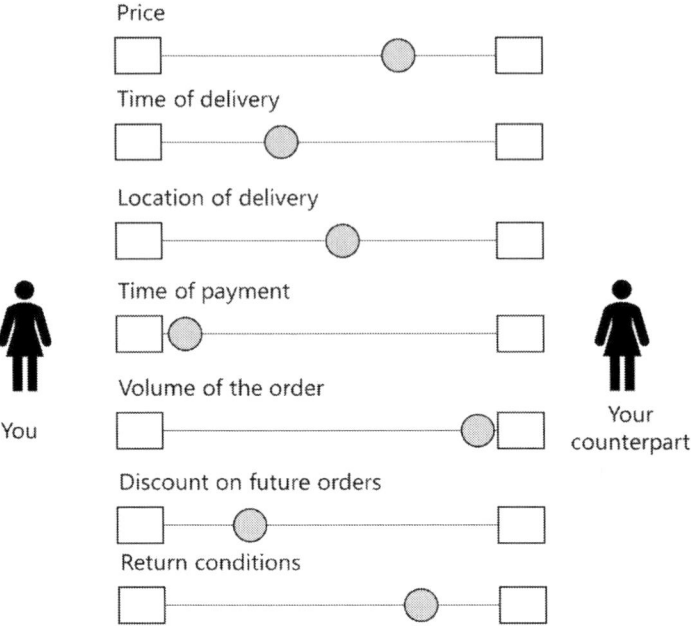

You are accepting a price closer to the wishes of your counterpart;
The time of delivery will be more convenient for you;
The location of the delivery will be somewhere in between;
The time of payment will be what you want (I guess "now");
The volume of the order will be what your counterpart wants (even 1 single piece);
The discount on future orders will be something closer to your wishes;

The return conditions will be closer to the wishes of your counterpart.

We could add several dimensions.
When you have several dimensions, two things happen:

First: it is no longer so easy to say who wins and who loses, since you win on some dimensions and you counterpart wins on other dimensions.

Second: maybe one dimension is very relevant for you and less relevant for your counterpart. You can choose which dimensions you want to win and which dimensions you don't care to win.

In this way you get what you really need, and both of you go back home satisfied to have won what both of you really wanted.

The books of management call this a "win-win" negotiated agreement.

Where is Harper?
Ok, here he is.
Before entering a negotiation, Harper prepares a multidimension solution and then he thinks about what is important for him and to what (he guesses) is important for the counterpart.

Then he enters the negotiation with a proposal that is "nice" for both parts. This is called "the going in position".

Some negotiations are not so symmetric.
There are some negotiations where one side is much stronger than the other one.
For example: you need someone with a good expertise on the software used in a company; you must integrate the software of that company. There is no one else able to do that.
This person is clearly in a stronger position than you.

What does Harper do? He realises he could receive a take or leave it proposal.

How much can we pay this person? 10.000 EUR? 50.000 EUR? 300.000 EUR?
This is a decision that must be shared with the board before entering the negotiation.

If we are victims of a blackmail, what do we decide to do?
How much are we willing to accept?
How much can we afford to pay?
Where is the threshold?
In the very worst-case scenario, when we cannot integrate the software of the company and we have

to copy all the data manually, how much will we spend in terms of money, time, risk of mistakes, etc.?

If the very worst-case scenario costs 500.000 EUR, Harper will enter the negotiation with this number in mind. If the request is lower than 500.000 EUR, he will accept. If the request is higher, he will leave.
Everyone was already aware of the possibility that we could be compelled to migrate the data manually, so no one will blame Harper for leaving the negotiation.

This threshold value, 500.000 EUR in our example, is called BATNA that is an acronym meaning Best Alternative To a Negotiated Agreement.

> You can use this acronym and tell your boss: «what is the BATNA for this negotiation? ». This will make you appear an expert of negotiations!

 **The movie corner**

The Negotiator
Directed by F. Gary Gray
USA 1998

This is a face to face confrontation between top negotiators for the Chicago Police Department. Listen very carefully to how they talk and what they do during the conversations.

 # Make this book your book

Think of a situation you lived where this competency is required

....
....

What did you do?

....
....

Think to someone you know that, in your opinion, masters this competency

....
....

What will you change / what will you do nest time?

....
....

Systemic thinking

The doctors are very familiar with the side effects that a drug can produce. Sometimes, when they have a patient, they compare the benefits that can derive by giving a drug with the disadvantages caused by the same drug as side effects.

This means that when we perform an action we must look at a higher horizon: we should not focus only on the immediate effect (which generally is good), but we must consider also the long term effect (which could be so bad to ruin the benefits produced before).

Sometimes the bad side effects can appear months later, i.e. there is a shift in time.
Sometimes they can appear in another organ, i.e. there is a shift in space.

We must look at a 360 degrees view both in space and in time.

We have to master the "what-if analysis".
This is the ability to imagine a situation in your mind even if you have never lived that situation before.

There is a very simple test to see if someone masters the what-if analysis or not. You can ask this question:

«What happens if a client tomorrow asks you for this product/service? »
Those who answer: «today clients don't ask for that product/service» they don't master the what-if analysis.

They cannot imagine a situation in the future different from the current situation, they need a concrete example to imagine a situation, they cannot think of something abstract.

> Let me give you a humble suggestion: never overestimate the number of people in a company that have the ability to think in abstract terms, you could be deeply disappointed.

Our friend, Oliver, will drive us through this competency.

1. Oliver masters what-if analysis.

2. When required, Oliver thinks in abstract terms.

3. Oliver thinks about the direct and indirect consequences on an action before accomplishing that action.

4. Oliver masters the complete feedback mechanism.

We have already detailed the first three points above. Let's focus on the fourth one. And let's think in abstract terms (we are in the right place!).

> Don't worry, later on we will provide a very practical and tangible example!

When you perform an action towards a system, the system responds with a result.

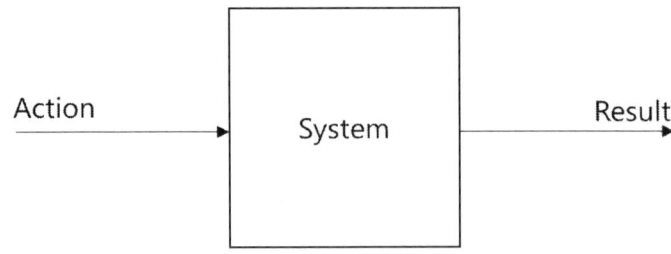

Example:
the system is: a business environment;

the action is: you increase the price of your products;
the result is: you increase your revenues (you sell the same number of products, at a higher price)

You know that this model is too simple to be true!

In the real (and complex) world, unfortunately there are no systems as simple as the one of the previous chart.
We must go at least to this level of complexity:

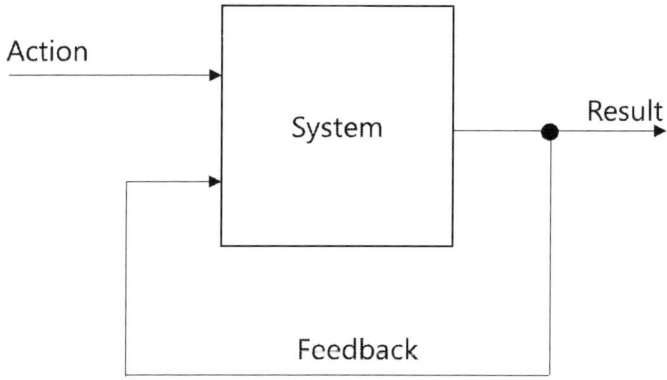

In this new chart, you see that a part of the result is drawn and sent back into the system together with the action. This is called the "feedback" loop, since this wire (that goes from the Result back to the input) "feeds" the system "backwards".

In some cases, this feedback is added to the action, so the overall input will be:
Action + Feedback
From a mathematical perspective, the Action and the Feedback have the same sign.

We call these cases "positive feedback" cases.

Here we mean "positive" in a mathematical sense: we have a sum since they have the same sign.

We are not giving any judgement to the feedback.

In other cases, the feedback is subtracted from the action, so the overall input will be:
Action - Feedback
From a mathematical perspective, the Action and the Feedback have the opposite sign.

We call these cases "negative feedback" cases.

Again, here we mean "positive" in a mathematical sense: we have a subtraction since they have the opposite sign.

Again, we are not giving any judgement to the feedback.

In our example, we reduce the price, the revenues increase but also the competitors reduce their prices… so our revenues stabilize.

This in example of "negative" feedback.

A negative feedback brings to a stabilization.

Another example: during a post merger integration project you merge the product catalogues of the two companies into just one product catalogue. This simplifies your procedures, your warehouse, etc. which will lead to a general cost reduction of 1 Million EUR that is, ultimately, an increase in earnings of 1 Million EUR[7].
Unfortunately, some clients could be disappointed and stop buying from you. You will experience a reduction in revenues of 1 Million EUR. The combination of the reduction in revenue and the (previous) reduction in costs stabilises the earnings. This is an example of negative feedback.

> I know what you are thinking: if the reduction of costs is smaller than the reduction of the revenues... this is not very good. This is an abstract example!

What about the positive feedback?
The positive feedback is tremendous!
It quickly brings to an extreme situation.

---

[7] *For the purpose of the example, let's use this very simple model:*
Revenues (the money a company receives from its clients)
- Costs (the money a company pays to its suppliers)
= Earnings (the money that remains in the company)

Typical example: during a time of crisis, people sell stocks (action). These sales push down the price of stocks (result).

A decrease in prices feeds back the system pushing more people to sell stocks (positive feedback).

If nothing intervenes to stop this positive feedback loop, the systems collapses (the prices go to zero!).

Generally, we do not like positive feedback loops!

 **The movie corner**

Dr. Strangelove
Directed by Stanley Kubrick
United Kingdom / USA 1964

This is a movie about the Cold War between the Soviet Union and the United States. In those years there was an escalation of nuclear weapons. The movie shows, in a satirical way, how to think about the implications of an action before doing it.

 # Make this book your book

Think of a situation you lived where this competency is required

....
....

What did you do?

....
....

Think to someone you know that, in your opinion, masters this competency

....
....

What will you change / what will you do nest time?

....
....

Situation awareness

This is the most difficult competency to define.
I would be tempted to say: «this competency encompasses everything that is not included in the other competencies».
I know this is not a good way of defining a competency. So, let's define it more seriously with Grace.

1. Grace understands quickly who the real decision maker in an organisation (or in a project) is.

2. Grace understands quickly what the complete flow of decisions is.

3. Grace knows when she must sing in the chorus and when she must go solo.

Let's see Grace at work with an example.

When Grace joined the company, she received the official org-chart, something like this:

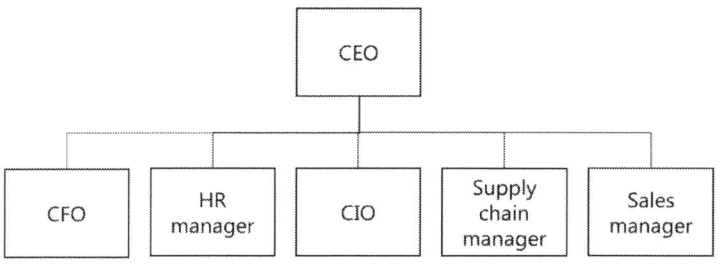

CEO = Chief Executive Officer
CFO = Chief Financial Officer
CIO = Chief Information Officer

During a meeting, Grace noticed that whenever the Supply chain manager suggested an idea, all the other managers agreed on this idea, even the CEO.

This means that the real decision maker in the company is the Supply chain manager, not the CEO. The official org-chart does not represent the real map of power.

This situation in a company (or in a project) is much more common than you can imagine.

There are several reasons, for example:
- a manager is much more senior than the other ones
- a manager entered the company before the other ones

- the nature of the business itself gives this manager more power
- a manager has a very close relationship with the owners of the company. Sometimes it can even be a family relationship.

It is not so important to understand the reason behind this situation, and even less important is to discuss if this situation is good for the company.

It is important to understand this situation very very quickly. Because every day you spend in the company before understanding it, is a day spent at high risk of stepping onto somebody's toes.

On a little higher level of complexity, Grace not only understands who the real decision maker is, she also understands the complete flow of the decision making.

Grace realises that, before taking any decision, the supply chain manager talks with the CFO.
This means that the CFO is a strong influencer; the Supply chain manager remains the real decision maker, but the CFO can impact the process of decision making.

When Grace entered the company, since the very beginning, she started behaving as everyone else,

she absorbed company culture very quickly, she became a woman of the company very soon.
This is what we call "sing in the chorus".
At the right moment in time, after talking to the right people in the right manner at the right time, she stood up and presented her idea during a very important meeting.
This is what we call "understand when you must go solo".

 **The movie corner**

The Devil Wears Prada
Directed by David Frankel
USA 2006

This is an iconic movie for the fashion and luxury business.
It is the story of a young woman who wants to work as a journalist. She applied for a job as an assistant to the editor-in-chief of a famous fashion magazine and she is hired even if she does not know anything about the fashion luxury business.

This is a perfect example of a person who does not have the situation awareness competency, but it is also a demonstration that competencies can be trained and improved.

 **Make this book your book**

Think of a situation you lived where this competency is required

....
....

What did you do?

....
....

Think to someone you know that, in your opinion, masters this competency

....
....

What will you change / what will you do nest time?

....
....

Multicultural thinking

Let's explore this competency with Sam.

1. Sam knows different cultures.

2. Sam reads different signals from the context and understands them accordingly to the culture.

3. Sam changes his behaviour depending on context.

Some people think that speaking more than one language is enough to master this competency. «I know Chinese, so I know Chinese culture, so I master multicultural thinking»

There are at least two mistakes in this thinking.

The first mistake is this: knowing a language does not imply automatically knowing the culture.
Of course, knowing the langue can help a lot; we say that this is necessary but not enough.

The second mistake is this: if some people know the culture, but they do not change their behaviour depending on the culture, then they are not mastering this competency.

 **The movie corner**

Lost in translation
Directed by Sofia Coppola
USA / Japan 2003

A very nice representation of the difficulties in "translating" the Japanese culture into the US culture and vice versa.

 # Make this book your book

Think of a situation you lived where this competency is required

....
....

What did you do?

....
....

Think to someone you know that, in your opinion, masters this competency

....
....

What will you change / what will you do nest time?

....
....

Focus on goal

1. Charlotte defines the goal clearly.

2. Charlotte gets the necessary "tools".

3. Charlotte eliminates the obstacles between her and the goal.

4. Charlotte gets excited in front of a difficulty.

5. Charlotte improves the results / process.

The first step is to define clearly the goal.
It could appear self-explaining, but our experience says that it is not always so!
If you want to focus on a goal, the first thing is to understand clearly what this goal is.

The second step is to get the right tools required to achieve the goal. Think "tools" in a broad sense: not only hammer and screwdriver! It depends on the situation.
They could be the right software and hardware tools.

Third step is the remove all the obstacles between you and the goal, to make the workflow smooth and fast.

When you meet Charlotte, you realise soon that she does her work as easy as pie. There is no magic in this. She removed all obstacles before starting her job.

Now we are entering the advanced level of mastering this competency.

Step four is for the high performing people. Charlotte is one of them!

It is a matter of approach: how do you approach a difficulty? Charlotte gets excited, she likes the challenge, she likes to achieve a goal. The higher the difficulty, the higher the pleasure in achieving it.

After achieving the goal, Charlotte does not stop. She thinks: «how could we do better next time? » and she writes it down. Time after time she will not only achieve the goal, but also achieve it in a faster, cheaper, more efficient and more effective way.

The movie corner

The Professor and the Madman
Directed by Farhad Safinia
USA / Ireland 2019

The film is about a professor who began compiling the Oxford English Dictionary at the end of the 19th century. In those years, writing a dictionary was a huge task (even today it is a big task, but today we have computers, internet, etc.). This professor is a very good example of the importance of staying focused on the goal.

 # Make this book your book

Think of a situation you lived where this competency is required

....
....

What did you do?

....
....

Think to someone you know that, in your opinion, masters this competency

....
....

What will you change / what will you do nest time?

....
....

Managing people

We are at the end of the list of the competencies. Now you know everything you need to manage your team. So, the last competency will be... managing people.

1. Evelyn tells her team members what to do.

2. Evelyn checks compliance with tasks / deadlines.

3. Evelyn solves performance issues.

4. Evelyn brings a positive attitude.

5. Evelyn provides mentoring to her team members.

Evelyn has already made a plan using her Planning competency (see the specific chapter for details). Now she has a chart with tasks and deadlines.

Evelyn tells her team members what they must do according to the plan. In doing so she must master her communication skills: listening to them, using the right language, etc. (see communication competency for the details).

Telling people what they must do and the deadlines, unfortunately, is not enough to have the tasks done.

> The sooner you accept this sad truth, the better!

People generally have a lot of things to do, emails to write, phone calls to answer, colleagues to meet, etc. all good and noble activities. Unfortunately, these activities are not part of the tasks of the project.

Evelyn knows this very well, so from time to time she checks with her team mates the achieved progress.
Again, in doing these checks she uses her communication competency: some of her team mates like to be checked and receive a feedback a couple of times a day (otherwise they feel abandoned), other team mates accept this check only once every other day (otherwise they feel micro-managed).

If Evelyn perceives some performance issues, she does what must be done to overcome these issues.

In doing all this, Evelyn never forgets to bring a positive attitude, and to mentor her teammates who ask her for mentoring.

Difficult enough? Yes, you are right!
Welcome to the real world of Post Merger Integration management.

 **The movie corner**

Hacksaw ridge
Directed by Mel Gibson
USA / Australia 2016

Sometimes a manager makes a mistake with a person of his team. A good manager admits his mistakes.

Gladiator
Directed by Ridley Scott
USA / United Kingdom 2000

A very famous movie. A masterpiece of leadership in managing people.

 # Make this book your book

Think of a situation you lived where this competency is required

....
....

What did you do?

....
....

Think to someone you know that, in your opinion, masters this competency

....
....

What will you change / what will you do nest time?

....
....

Part 3:
Cases & Exercises

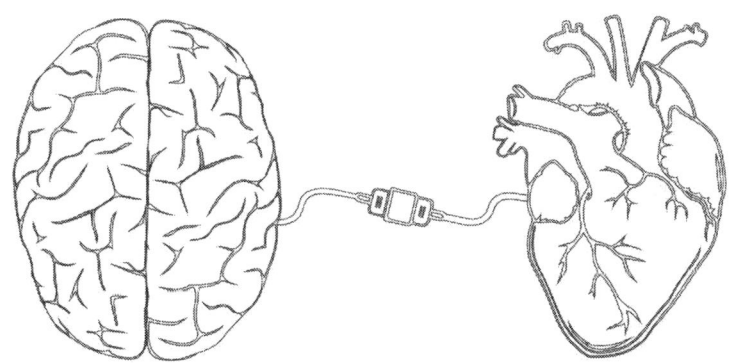

Robert and the new boss

Situation

Robert is the owner of a company. He owns 100% of the company. The company was founded by his grandfather, then was inherited by his father and then by him.
Now Robert sells the company. He remains in the company because he loves it, he remembers when he used to come to his father's office when he was a child.
The day after he sold the company, he moves from being the owner to being an employee. He is no longer the decision maker. He must report to a CEO. Today it is the first day he goes to the office as an employee, no longer as an owner. Robert used to work late hours, he used to spend some time with his family, go to the office mid-Morning, and then come back home late, around 10 PM. Days later, in a meeting, he realises his colleagues were talking about him. He is not respecting the standard working hours that everyone else follows: 9AM to 1PM and then 2PM to 6 PM. His colleagues accuse him of being always late. He answers he is working more than them since he is always the last one to

leave the office. His colleagues tell him he must behave as all the other managers do, he must be part of the team, he must stop being "a voice out of the chorus". Robert thinks it is a joke, since today it is April 1st. Unfortunately, it is not…

Robert's life changed in one day. Of course, he expected this change. But he could never imagine it would have happened this way.

Questions

- How does he feel?

- How are you expecting his feelings will affect his performance?

- What could you do as a manager to manage his feelings in order to keep his performance and engagement?

Susan in the matrix

Situation

A company, with a traditional hierarchical structure, is acquired by a large company with a matrix organization.

In a traditional hierarchical structure, Susan has one (and only one) well identified boss. In each moment, whatever the task is, Susan knows exactly whom to report to.

A matrix organisation is much more complex.

In a matrix organisation, Jennifer that works in Sales in Canada has two bosses: one is the global head of Sales, the other one is the country manager of Canada.
The picture below, shows this matrix:

		Functions				
		Finance	Human Resources	Information Technology	Supply Chain	Sales
Countries	UK					
	USA					
	Germany					
	Canada					Jennifer
	France					
	Italy					
	China					
	Belgium					
	Sweden					

What you just saw is a two-dimensions matrix: Functions and Countries.

I forgot to tell you that there is also another dimension: the product line.
The new company has three product lines:
- Food
- Home care
- Personal care

Jennifer works in Canada (country) in the Sales (function) of Food (product).

With some creativity you could imagine this three-dimensions matrix, and the three bosses of Jennifer.

I also forgot to tell you that there is a fourth dimension: the client segment.
The company has three client segments:
- Retail
- HORECA[8]
- Large distribution

Jennifer works in the Retail segment, so she reports also to the Retail boss.
I also forgot to tell you...
No, this time I was joking. Jennifer has only 4 bosses since she works in a company that has 4 dimensions.

Then there is the merger.
The two companies become one.
The merged company will have a matrix organisation.
Susan and Jennifer will work together.

Questions

- How does Susan feel?

- How are you expecting her feelings will affect her performance?

---

[8] *HORECA is an acronym that means: Hotel, Restoration, Catering*

- What could you do as a manager to manage her feelings in order to keep her performance and engagement?

Who is Thomas?

Situation

Thomas is the CFO of a company.
When someone asks him: «what's your job? ». He answers: «I'm a CFO».
He never answered: «I work as a CFO».

I am not splitting hairs, but the way Thomas answers reveal that the job he does contributes deeply to his individual identity.
This is very common. Even our language has a widely used form that overlaps the identity of the person with the job.
Of course, in these cases, if you change something in the job (perhaps during an M&A organization change), you are changing their perception of their own individual identity.

We all know that changing your car is very easy, changing your opinions is not so difficult, but changing your habits or ignoring your feelings during a big change is almost impossible.

Questions

- How does Thomas feel?

- How are you expecting his feelings will affect his performance?

- What could you do as a manager to manage his feelings in order to keep his performance and engagement?

Bob & Jane

Situation

Bob is the head of sales of a company that sells retail products and deliver them to the final client.
There has just been a merger and the company has now a new system for organising the delivery of the orders.
Jane is a client; she made an order one week ago and yesterday she received something she did not order.
Jane calls the customer service and complains.
The customer service takes note of the fact she did not receive what she ordered, then the customer service organises a new delivery for the product Jane ordered and finally a return of the wrong product.

Bob sees what the customer service did and is happy with that.

Questions

- Is this problem solving?

- In other words: do you see that the customer service and Bob did all the actions listed under the problem solving competency?

- If not, what else should they do?

Can we have Abhishek back?

Situation

Abhishek is the Chief Information Officer (CIO) of the company ABC.
He started working in ABC just after graduating in computer science from the Massachusetts Institute of Technology (MIT). He followed all the major Information Technology projects in ABC. He is the only one in the company that knows everything about the Information Technology systems of ABC.

«XYZ will acquire ABC» Abhishek hears this rumour. It is only a rumour. Nothing official. We are still in that time when there are only rumours. People would really like to know the truth, the final truth… but they only have nothing more than rumours.

One day, Tanya, one of Abhishek colleagues tells him that she is going to leave ABC in one week. She doesn't know yet if the acquisition will happen or not, but she is afraid to lose her job after the acquisition (if it will happen one day).

As soon as the news of Tanya leaving the firm spreads, other 3 colleagues leave the firm. All of them for the same reason.

Questions

- From a systemic perspective, are we facing a positive feedback system or a negative feedback system?

- If we do nothing what could happen?

- Could we complete the post merger integration without Abhishek?

- If Abhishek what could we do to have him back?

- In these situations, where there are rumours that Abhishek's company is going to be acquired, who are the people who will find a new job more quickly and will leave the company sooner?

How to choose your team

Situation

You are the Program manager of the integration project. You need someone who takes care of a specific area, you have two options: one is Tom, the other one is John.
Which one will you choose?
Based on what?

Solution

Of course, you can use your gut feeling! Never under-estimate the power of gut feeling! But sometimes we need something more scientific. You can base your decision on this scientific approach, or you can follow your gut feeling and use the scientific approach to confirm or deny it. Or you can use the scientific approach (without telling anybody you are using it) and then you declare that you choose Tom instead of Bob based on your gut feeling. This last approach is the one I see more often!

We could debate for hours about why executives sometimes prefer to say they base their decision on a gut feeling instead of a scientific approach, but this is not the topic of this book!

Let's stick with our agenda: how can you use these competencies in a scientific way to choose your teammates for your project? Is Tom better than John?

This is the process:

Step 1:
Take the list of competencies and give a weight to each one of them. You can give a weight based on how much you think this competency is relevant in this specific project or in this specific environment.

You can use the following weight system:
- This competency is fundamental → weight = 3
- This competency is not so relevant in this case → weight = 1
- This competency is important but not fundamental → weight = 2

At the end of this step you will have a table like this one:

Competency	Weight
Problem solving	1
Planning	2
Communication	3
Negotiation	3
Systemic thinking	3
Situation awareness	1
Multicultural thinking	1
Focus on goal	2
Managing people	2

There is also a shortcut: you can say that the weight is 3 for all the competencies.

This option has two advantages:
Saves you some time

Makes you think that, by doing so, you can advertise that your project is really very difficult (and, as long as other people believe you, your advertisement will be successful)

Step 2:
You take the list of actions that define a competency. For example, you take the list of actions that define the competency "Problem Solving".

Step 3:
Then you think of Tom and ask yourself: «does Tom do action #1? ». The answer could be: "yes" "no" "sometimes". You can set a score for each answer, for example:
- Yes = 10
- No = 0
- Sometimes = 5

If you like to give your work a truly scientific look and feel, you can also use scores like 6.6 (meaning that Tom does action #1 a bit more often than "sometimes") or 3.14 (meaning that Tom does action #1 a bit more often than "never"). Here we will keep it simple and use only 10,5,0.

Now you should have a table like this:

N.	Action	Score of Tom
1.	Bob analyses the situation	5
2.	Bob puts on the table a set of potential solution	10
3.	Bob evaluates pros and cons of each potential solution	10
4.	Bob makes a decision that is he pick one potential solution	5
5.	Bob checks if the solution he picked solves the problem. If not, he iterates from the beginning	5
6.	Bob checks if the problem was a one-off problem or a recurring problem	0
7.	If it is a recurring problem, then Bob ensures that, with the solution he picked, this problem will not show in the future. If not, he iterates from the beginning	0
8.	Once Bob found the final solution, he writes down what he did.	5
	TOTAL SCORE	40
	AVERAGE SCORE	5.0

The average score is the total score divided by the number of actions. In this case, it is 40 divided by 8 that is 5.0.

Step 4:
You do the same for all other competencies.

At this point you should have a table like this:

Competency	Score of Tom
Problem solving	5.0
Planning	2.6
Communication	8.2
Negotiation	6.0
Systemic thinking	5.1
Situation awareness	3.0
Multicultural thinking	2.0
Focus on goal	2.9
Managing people	9.5

Step 5:
You do the same for John and you get a table like this:

Competency	Score of John
Problem solving	5.5
Planning	6.2
Communication	7.2
Negotiation	6.8
Systemic thinking	5.5
Situation awareness	3.9
Multicultural thinking	2.9
Focus on goal	2.0
Managing people	8.5

Step 6:

Do you remember what you did centuries ago in Step1? (yeah, I know it feels like a century ago!). you gave a weight to each competency. You said that not all the competencies are at the same level of importance. This means that if John beats Tom on *problem solving* but Tom beats John on *communication*, you must see if *problem solving* is more or less important than *communication* in order to make a decision.

There is a trick: you multiply the scores of Tom on each competency by the weight of each competency, for example *problem solving* score is 5.0 (from Step4) and you multiply it by 1 (from Step1).

This is what you get:

Competency	Weighted Score of Tom	Weighted Score of John
Problem solving	5	5.5
Planning	5.2	12.4
Communication	24.6	21.6
Negotiation	18	20.4
Systemic thinking	15.3	16.5
Situation awareness	3	3.9
Multicultural thinking	2	2.9
Focus on goal	5.8	4
Managing people	19	17

And now you just sum up all the weighted scores and you get 97.7 for Tom and 104.2 for John, which leads to the conclusion that, on this specific project, in this specific moment in time, John is more suitable than Tom.

I would like to drive your attention once more towards these two sentences:
- *"in this specific project"*
- *"in this specific moment in time"*

Please, don't ever forget that this result was a consequence of the weights that you gave to each competency. If you take another project, in a different situation, you will probably give different weights to the competencies and the result sill probably different, that is Tom can fit better than John.

"in this specific moment in time" Yes! The score of Tom and of John can change with time. Maybe Tom starts doing an action more often, this will increase his score. Maybe John gets bored of doing something, stops doing it and this will lower his score. Who knows?
Why should John stop his performing behaviour? Good question. To answer this question, we will have to go through the chapter of his motivation, his engagement with the project. Nothing "strange" if his level of engagement changes with time; just be aware of the fact that it can change and be ready to take the right countermeasures.

How can Tom increase his score?

I like this question! This shows the fact that Tom wants to become a manager / employee that fits our project better.

> This also gives me the opportunity to sell a good training course on how to develop management competencies. But we generally do not say this too

loud. We prefer to focus on the fact that Tom demonstrated a good approach towards his job.

The answer is: «yes there is a way», and this will be our next case exercise.

How to improve your team

Situation

You have a budget to spend on training for your manager, Mary, and you would like to spend it in the most effective way since you need to prepare them for a near future integration. How should you procced?

Solution

Step 1:
Again, let's start from our list of competencies:

Competency
Problem solving
Planning
Communication
Negotiation
Systemic thinking
Situation awareness
Multicultural thinking
Focus on goal
Managing people

Step 2:
For each competency you will give a score: it is the score that Mary should have in order to cover the role you have in mind for her in the best way.

The output will be something like this:

Competency	Expected score
Problem solving	5
Planning	10
Communication	10
Negotiation	5
Systemic thinking	7
Situation awareness	8
Multicultural thinking	0
Focus on goal	5
Managing people	2

This is specific for the job you have in mind. In the example we see that the expected score for the competency "Multicultural thinking" is 0. This means that multicultural thinking for this job is not important. We are not saying that it is not important in general: it is not important for this specific job, maybe because everybody belongs to the same culture, so there is no need of a high score on this competency.

Step 3:
Now focus on Mary and give her a score on each competency (you learned how to do in the previous case-exercise).

You will get a new table like this:

Competency	Score of Mary
Problem solving	5
Planning	6.1
Communication	2.7
Negotiation	6.8
Systemic thinking	7.5
Situation awareness	9
Multicultural thinking	6.2
Focus on goal	5.2
Managing people	8.5

Step 4:
Put the score of Mary close to the expected score:

Competency	Expected score	Score of Mary
Problem solving	5	5
Planning	10	6.1
Communication	10	2.7
Negotiation	5	6.8
Systemic thinking	7	7.5
Situation awareness	8	9
Multicultural thinking	0	6.2
Focus on goal	5	5.2
Managing people	2	8.5

Let's see what we have here.

- Problem solving: OK
- Planning: mmm, less than expected: training needed.
- Communication: same as Planning
- Negotiation: OK
- Systemic Thinking: OK
- Situation Awareness: OK
- Multicultural thinking: much more than expected. It's is a pity; we will not exploit this competency of Mary on this project.
- Focus on goal: OK
- Managing people: same as Multicultural thinking.

So, the answer is: use your budget to train Mary on Planning and Communication.

> If you do not want to go through all this, you can ask an external consultant to do it. The consultant will evaluate Mary in the most objective way. Just by chance, Mary will happen to have a score lower than expected on the competencies where the external consultant has a very good training material ready.

If you really want to exceed the expectations of your boss, you could think a little about the two competencies that Mary has and that you will not use on this project (Multicultural Thinking and Managing people). What happens if Mary does not use these competencies on this project? Most likely she will get worse...

The question for you is maybe Mary will come to you one day and tell you: «One year ago, I was very good in managing people, but now, working on this new job, I feel I'm losing this competency. I do not like this job anymore».

You told me you wanted to exceed the expectations of your boss, didn't you?
So, you'd better start thinking about someone else who could take Mary's role, just to be prepared in case she comes to you with this question.

 **Essential Bibliography**

Blustein, David L. *The Psychology of Working: A New Perspective for Career Development, Counseling, and Public Policy.* Routledge, 2006

Bradberry, Travis and Greaves, Jean. *Emotional Intelligence 2.0.* TalentSmart, 2009

Burgo, Joseph. *Shame: Free Yourself, Find Joy, and Build True Self-Esteem.* St. Martin's Essentials, 2018

Burgo, Joseph. *Why Do I Do That?: Psychological Defense Mechanisms and the Hidden Ways They Shape Our Lives.* New Rise Press, 2013

Burrough, Bryan and Helyar, John. *Barbarians at the Gate: The Fall of RJR Nabisco.* Harper Business, 2008

Chapman, Gary and White, Paul. *The 5 Languages of Appreciation in the Workplace: Empowering Organizations by Encouraging People.* Northfield Publishing, 2019

Coffey, Adam. *The Private Equity Playbook: Management's Guide to Working with Private Equity.* Lioncrest Publishing, 2019

Covey, Stephen M.R. *The speed of trust, The Speed of Trust: The One Thing that Changes Everything.* FranklinCovey, 2006

Csikszentmihalyi, Mihaly. *Flow: The Psychology of Optimal Experience.* HarperCollins, 2008

Cunningham, Lawrence A. *Margin of Trust: The Berkshire Business Model.* Columbia Business School, 2020

Fisher, Roger and Ury, William L. *Getting to Yes: Negotiating Agreement Without Giving In.* Penguin Books, 2011

Goleman, Daniel. *Emotional Intelligence.* Bantam Books, 1995
Jobs, Steve. *Commencement address.* Stanford University, 2005

Kahneman, Daniel and Egan, Patrick. *Thinking, Fast and Slow.* Farrar, Straus and Giroux, 2011

Kerzner, Harold. *Project Management: A Systems Approach to Planning, Scheduling, and Controlling*. Wiley, 2017

Kets de Vries, Manfred F.R. and Balazs, Katharina. *The Downside of Downsizing*. Human Relations, 1997

Kotler, Philip. *Marketing Management: Analysis, Planning and Control*. Prentice Hall International, 1996 [the first edition was published in 1967]

Meadows, Donella H. and Wright, Diana. *Thinking in Systems*. Chelsea Green Publishing, 2008

Meyr, Erin. *The Culture Map*. Pubblic Affairs, 2015
Organ, Dennis W. *Organizational Citizenship Behavior: The Good Soldier Syndrome*. Lexington Books, 1988

Pink, Daniel H. *Drive: The Surprising Truth About What Motivates Us*. Riverhead Books, 2009

Poniachek, Harvey A. *Mergers & Acquisitions:A Practitioner's Guide to Successful Deals*. World Scientific Publishing, 2019

Rosenbaum, Joshua and Pearl, Joshua. *Investment Banking: Valuation, Leveraged Buyouts, and Mergers and Acquisitions*. Wiley, 2013

Schabracq, Marc J.; Winnubst, Jacques A. M.; Cooper, Cary. *The Handbook of Work and Health Psychology*. Wiley, 2002

Schoeck, Helmut. *Envy: A Theory of Social Behaviour*. Liberty Fund, 1987

Senge, Peter M. *The Fifth Discipline: The Art and Practice of the Learning Organization*. Doubleday Business, 1990

Sweeney, Patrick J. *Fear Is Fuel: The Surprising Power to Help You Find Purpose, Passion, and Performance*. Rowman & Littlefield, 2020

Taleb, Nassim Nicholas. *Skin in the Game: Hidden Asymmetries in Daily Life*. Random House, 2018

Warrillow, John. *Built to Sell: Creating a Business That Can Thrive Without You*. Portfolio, 2011

Welch, Jack and Byrne, John. *Jack: Straight from the Gut*. Grand Central Publishing, 2003

Whitaker, Scott and other contributors. *Cross-Border Mergers and Acquisitions.* Wiley, 2016

Whitaker, Scott. *Mergers & Acquisitions Integration Handbook: Helping Companies Realize the Full Value of Acquisitions.* Wiley, 2012

Printed in Great Britain
by Amazon